DIARY OF A

Goal

Digger

CHIARA GRAHAM

Credits
Editorial: Carla DuPont
Cover Design: Justin Foster
Interior Design: Carla DuPont

CONTENTS

iv

DIARY OF A

Goal

Digger

DO YOU KNOW YOUR
Why

All organizations, businesses, and careers generally operate on three standards: WHAT we do, HOW we do it, and WHY we do it. And well, don't you treat yourself like a business or a brand? As famed rapper and entrepreneur Jay-Z said, "I'm not a businessman, I'm a business man. We all have a pretty good indication of what we want to do. Then there's having an idea of how to get it done. However, the last standard, 'why' is where many of us fail to be able to clearly articulate our personal motivation behind the 'what'.

Why is the purpose, cause, or belief that drives you. Why does your goal exist? Why do you get out of bed in the morning? Why should anyone else care about what you're doing? Why do you want to succeed?

Your why is what separates you from the crowd. It is a purpose that inspires you to action. If powerful enough, your why can also inspire others to move. Few things in life give a person inner peace like knowing what fulfills them. Fulfillment is something we are entitled to by birth, not a privilege. Finding fulfillment begins with knowing and understanding why you set goals and why you do what you do.

As you come into understanding your why, then you will be able to better articulate how your why brings fulfillment, as well as how you behave when naturally performing at optimal levels. This gives you a point of reference as you make decisions and move forward into productive spaces. You will act and make choices based on intention regarding all aspects of your business and career, but especially your life's goals. Intention leads to dedication, both of which are infectious when rallying support for others to join you or help you.

On our personal journeys, we seek wisdom, fulfillment, peace, knowledge, and meaning. "Why am I here?" we ask ourselves trying to find a purpose in all of this. Most of us crave purpose and abundance, two things we can probably all agree on. We try to get a sense of purpose by spreading ourselves over a ton of activities we are obligated to do such as work and family relationships. A few people even take much needed time away from their usual circle of people and activities trying to find themselves. High school graduates are increasingly taking a 'gap year' between high school and college to discover who they are, and people take extended trips to foreign countries for the same reason.

As we get older, allowing maturity to find us, we can arrange our schedules to work in our favor in an attempt to provide ourselves the life we desire, inclusive of our loved ones' schedules and desires. Before jumping out to act on something, we want to know why, then, we try to measure the intended outcome. If the why stimulates us enough and the intended outcome seems obtainable, then we feel that acting on it will bring value and fulfillment to our lives.

Why Do You Do What You Do

If only figuring out your why were as easy as rubbing a crystal ball, right? It really shouldn't be that difficult to find. To get somewhere, you have to know where you want to end up. The sooner you define your end goal, the easier and more clear the journey will become. Thomas Oppong said, A life without a purpose is a life without a destination." With a little concentrated thought and effort, you will be able to see vividly the reasoning behind your thoughts and actions. True, there is a little fear in finding success in becoming who you are meant to be; however, the rewards are priceless.

Are you ready to live a life on your terms? Do you want to have clarity? Are you serious about attaining those goals you have bursting out of your mind? Do you seek more peace and confidence creating goals for you that will bring your greater fulfillment? Look at these categories to help determine your why.

➢ *Obligation (Need)*

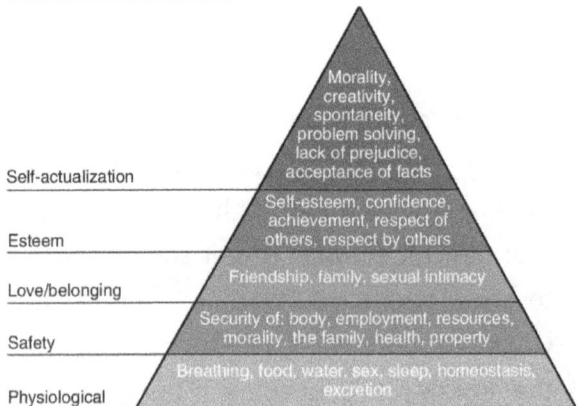

Abraham   Maslow's   Hierarchy   of   Needs.   Source: https://www.researchgate.net/figure/Maslows-1943-hierarchy-of-needs-From-Open-source-Creative-Commons_fig1_286501602

At the base of Maslow's Hierarchy of Needs pyramid, we find obligation which consists of our most fundamental needs. Food, water, clothing, and shelter, are among things we need simply to survive. We can provide them for ourselves, or they can be provided by others or even the government.

There are luxuries, then there are necessities. We work to provide them both; however, the necessities must come first. We aim to keep a roof over our heads and food in our bellies. Whether having these provisions is a conscious thought or not, we do what we have to do to survive, as well as provide obligations to those who depend on us.

➤ *Pride (Sense of duty)*

A sense of duty or pride is a broad range of beliefs and actions from patriotism to nationalism to volunteerism. It is pledging ourselves to a cause we deem greater than ourselves. There is a call to action within each belief that others benefit from the very acts we take pride in. The fruits of our labor produce a feeling of a job well done.

➤ *Vice (Selfish intention)*

Sometimes we act in ways that seem to be in our best interest when really we are only going to receive temporary pleasure and/or long-term pain. Vices are selfish and don't benefit us in any way. Usually, vices are the things we should avoid. Don't feel bad, we all have them and we all act on them. Vices are also distractions that we should avoid.

➢ *Love (For the Benefit of Others)*
Committing acts of kindness, or altruism is a gift that will be reciprocated. There are people in our lives who we would do anything for. Seeing a smile brought to these faces gives us a greater sense of purpose and helps us to feel rewarded ourselves. Some of the most beautiful actions and intentions are based on loving one another.

➢ *Passion*
A passion for me is helping others to achieve their goals. It is something I love to do and does not feel like work even when the person who I am helping feels overwhelmed and confused. Bringing a sense of peace to them, along with direction fulfills my urge to feel needed. And I'm good at it. I offer encouragement and guidance to others to help them which gives me a tremendous sense of pride. I desire to have a positive influence on them. That's what passion is all about, spending

the time and doing the work on things that bring us enthusiasm.

➢ *Mission Accomplished*

Sometimes we just want to do something so we can say we did it, not that we necessarily get satisfaction from the act itself. Bucket list items, gaining a degree or certificate, or learning a new skill that you probably won't put to much use and certainly won't earn any money doing, fall in this category. But, guess what? You did it! And it could lead to something more profitable than self-fulfillment down the road.

➢ *Destiny*

Your mother may be a teacher, your aunts, uncles, and cousins are teachers. You adjust the bar for yourself, wanting to do something different, yet in the end find yourself standing in front of a classroom. It could be destiny that your why is tied into and you can't escape that.

➢ *For Show (Attention and Affection)*

As humans, it is natural to desire affection and attention from others. To gain it, you may find yourself in some pretty interesting situations that you wouldn't normally be in.

Particularly where romance is involved. Some act out in class or at family functions to get a rise out of everyone because they love the attention. Look at your actions to see if you act a certain way to get a certain response. You may be surprised by the result.

➢ *For Us (Self-Actualization and Fulfillment)*
To reach an important goal, we have to really want it. Through the journey, we need to feel energized, encouraged and empowered to get to the end. As we work to get there, we evolve as individuals, and emerge happy, fulfilled, and with a stronger belief in ourselves. Those around us cheering for us see our transformation and seek to find one of their own in one way or another. Even though others see our wins, sometimes they really are just for us.

The Right Time To Find Your Why

By this point in your life, surely you have encountered a significant crisis. It is during those times that we summon the energy we thought was tapped out and unparalleled determination to find a solution. We, all of a sudden, have the courage that we didn't even know was inside of us. Your goal is clear; focus is precise. You knew what your why was. There is no one pathway to discovering the why behind your goal. Perhaps, your why is tied into the goal itself, meaning the why is what prompted you to set the goal in the first place.

What about during times when life is trucking along and there isn't a seriously impending deadline or doom ahead of you to drive you to operate within a purpose. What is motivating you to keep going on the road ahead? This is the perfect time to find your why.

How about when you are feeling stuck? When you're looking for a more enriching lifestyle or meaningful work? This is the perfect time to find your why.

Your Why Statement
Your why statement is a way to clearly communicate your purpose to yourself and others. Think along the lines of a business elevator pitch. Your why statement should be clear and concise, like really concise, only a sentence or two. In the grand scheme of things, your why should be evergreen, meaning it can be applied to both personal and professional aspects of your life.

In Simon Sinek's *Find Your Why*, he and his co-authors say your why statement "is a statement of your value at work as much as it is the reason your friends love you. We don't have a professional WHY and personal WHY. We are who we are wherever we are. Your contribution is not a product or a service. It's the thing around which everything you do— the decisions you make, the tasks you perform, the products you sell— aligns to bring about the impact you envision."

Simon et al have come up with a quick strategy to writing a why statement.

TO _____ SO THAT _____.

The first space signifies your contribution to the lives of others through your why. The second space represents the impact of your contribution. Simon's why statement is, *"To inspire people to do the things that inspire them so that, together, we can change our world."*

My why statement is,

_____

Now, it's your turn to draft your own why statement.

1. Grab a pad and pen and write down, "TO _____ SO THAT _____" template. Keep in mind, there is no right or wrong way to write this statement. Be true to who you are and the rest will follow. Also, keep in mind this statement can always change.

2. Draft as many why statements as you need to until you find the one that resonates with you the most.

3. Cheers yourself! You've found your why!

Confidence

Are you intimidated by other's success?

Do you have a personal mantra?

Do you dress for the position you want?

Have you accepted you for you?

Do you take pride in yourself as much as your business?

Do you compare yourself to others?

"You gotta have confidence!" is one of the most common phrases you will hear, especially when branching out to begin something new. If you are honest with yourself, you know whether or not you are confident in your day-to-day. When you are goal-minded, being confident is a critical trait to have.

What Is Confidence Anyway?

By Merriam-Webster's definition, confidence is a feeling or consciousness of one's powers or reliance on one's circumstances. Another way to put it, confidence is knowing the value you bring, what you're good at, and carrying yourself in a way that displays both of those to others. Now, this is different than arrogance or conceit which is where you think you are better than you really are and downing others because of it. A good way to think of confidence is, it is smack in the middle of arrogance and low self-esteem. You know what you bring to the table and are being assured in yourself that you are just the right person to bring it because either you've done it or feel *confident* that you will be able to.

Confidence is not just thinking overly positive about yourself. It is a quality that is so important in every aspect of our lives, still, some struggle to find it. Think about the people you know around you who you view as successful. Do they seem confident in themselves and their abilities? Think about someone who you follow on social media, do they seem confident in their talents? It seems that most successful people have a confidence in themselves. It helps them to achieve their goals and encourages others to be drawn to them whether it's charismatic confidence or more quiet confidence. Some people just have what it takes to make you believe in them as much as they believe in themselves.

A good example of this is to think about a small candle business. If someone was trying to talk you into purchasing a candle from their company and fumbled over the candle jars while nervously saying, "Well...you should buy my candles because they do smell good. Kinda. And the burn time is alright, I guess," you would probably walk away. You would instantly know that they were not confident in their product versus a pitch like, "Let me introduce you to my amazing soy candles! They are made to smell like your favorite delectable desserts and burn for hours and hours." Hours and hours could only be four hours, but the pitch made you a believer that you should invest in this small candle company.

When you have confidence, it shows. Physically, you take pride in the way you dress, how your hair looks, and your personal hygiene is up to par. You are clean and well put together. Personality-wise, you carry yourself differently. There seems to be an air about yourself. In talking to people, your speech is clear, you hold your head high, and hold conversations with confidence. Even if you don't know the answer, you are confident in admitting as such.

Are You Intimidated By Other's Success?
Do you see the way some people work the room and wish you had that same effect on others? Do you watch them inspire others and it seems like you could say the same thing, but not demand the

same outcome? It seems like when those people speak, they can easily persuade their audience to see things their way. Believe it or not, gaining the confidence of others is one of the ways that illustrate how a confident person finds success. Has one of your friends started a podcast and you've been dying to start one? Perhaps one of your friends recently got married and now you're looking at your boyfriend with the side-eye.

Though there are many factors at play in the jealousy of others' success including who it is, what they have accomplished, and what you have going on in your life at the time, you may not be all that happy for them accomplishing a goal of theirs. You may be excited and inspired for them while at the same time feel a tinge of jealousy and intimidation come up. If they become successful at something you've been wanting, or even trying to do, you may experience a bit of inferiority complex.

You have to be real with yourself and what you are feeling. As social beings, we are intended to be influencers or to be influenced. It is only natural to notice and react to someone else's milestones. Status, power, and success are those milestones. A shift in your mindset will help to keep those reactions from being negative.

Get down to the root of why their success intimidates you. I'll tell you in one word...fear. You were afraid to go get your own success. Fear takes over and competes with your rational thinking. It keeps you from believing in yourself or, being confident in who you are. Ask yourself what *exactly* are you afraid of. What is it about seeing someone else win that causes your insecurities to come to the surface?

Do You Compare Yourself To Others?

Well, yes? If their success causes you to get in your feelings, you are certainly comparing yourself to them. You look at them and think, "Dang, Michelle is over there killing it while I'm stuck in the same place as I was two years ago." What makes comparisons stab us even deeper is because we are comparing their strengths to our weaknesses. We look at their wins and compare them to our losses. That is apples to oranges. Yes, we all do it; however, some of us do it more often than others.

That is a recipe for unhappiness and keeps us from finding success in our own lives. Comparing yourself to others will never be a fair comparison. There are far too many unknowns. You have only a slight idea of what their journey has looked like to get to the win you openly see.

If you compared strengths to strengths, guess what? One of you would still come out on top. Someone will always be number one. That is why for every sport you have, there is a reigning champion at the end of the season and in sales, a salesperson who ranks number one in the store, then in the district, and ultimately in the company.

Get out of comparing yourself to others by:

> *Being aware.* It's natural to compare and sometimes we don't even realize we are doing it. Be conscious of when you sell yourself short by comparing yourself to others. Being conscious that you're doing it is the first step to stopping this damaging behavior.

> *Take a pause.* When you realize you are comparing yourself, pause that thought. Don't make yourself feel bad for doing it, just shift your focus.

> *Focus on your strengths.* The first thing we do in comparison is to bring attention to

where we lack. Instead, do just the opposite. Focus on what you do well. Celebrate the progress you have made and use that to fuel the #goaldigging you have to do.

➢ ***Be ok with your imperfections.*** Not a single one of us is perfect, even though some would like you to think they are, LOL! While we know this in our heads, it's a little harder convincing our hearts. Spend more energy on improving who and where you are. You're not perfect, neither am I. Simply strive to be a better version of yourself.

Accept Yourself For Who You Are

We have all made mistakes and certainly missed some great opportunities. But, dwelling on these will not bring the time or the opportunities back to us. To be honest, you are probably more accepting of others' flaws and shortcomings than you are of your own. That is why the popular saying, "We are our own worst critics" often rings true.

Self-acceptance can be hard especially because you may be holding on to an altered version of your reality. We fantasize about the house we want, the car we want, the partner we want, and the job...or lack thereof...that we want. But when we shake ourselves back to the present, we look at the apartment we live in, the ten-year-old domestic car we drive, an empty bed, and the same work-life and wonder why they are so different. Then get sad because they are so different.

You can never be happy or flourish where you are if you are constantly waiting for the next thing. The next promotion, the next launch, the next win. Doing this will keep you looking at where you are as it is unfulfilling. Facing where you are may not be the easiest thing to do, but finding happiness in the present helps you to move forward with greater intention. You won't feel so rushed to move forward that you miss critical steps that lead to mistakes that actually set you further behind. You also won't let the success of others beat you down to where you focus more on their wins than spending quality time preparing for your own glow-up.

Once you accept where and who you are, you can confidently plan to do better. Instead of saying, "I hate my body and the way I look. I could never wear a bathing suit like that," rephrase it as, "This is how much I weigh and the status of my health. If

I want to confidently wear a bathing suit like that, these are the steps I need to take to lose weight." No matter what the goal is, steps must be outlined to help guarantee your chances of succeeding at that goal.

Show Your Confidence

When you are confident in yourself, it shows in everything you do. You will make a genuine effort at whatever it is that you are doing, or you won't do it at all. It's not that you are striving to be perfect, but rather looking for opportunities to relay your talents. It could be helping your child with homework, planting a garden at your house, or putting on a webinar for new clients; if you are going to do it, you want to do it well.

When you are confident in yourself, you also are more willing to help others. If you see someone falling short in an arena you are familiar with and you want to help them do better, you'll jump at the chance to help them. When I see someone trying to set a goal for themselves and they are struggling with the steps to take, I jump right in to help them. The effects of reaching out to help others can be long-lasting.

Being sure of yourself, who you are and what you represent, sets the standard for how you are treated. Friends, family, and co-workers will know that they can't just walk over you or treat you any kind of way. If you aren't confident in yourself as a person, what will make them want to?

Here are 10 ways to work on your confidence!

➢ Fix the things you don't like about yourself.

➢ Explain something you understand very well.

➢ Learn power poses.

➢ Dress better.

➢ Learn how to put on make-up.

➢ Work out and eat healthier.

➢ Practice when there is nothing at stake.

➢ Listen to music.

➢ Accept compliments...and give them to strangers!

➢ Learn a new skill.

Some say, "Fake it 'til you make it." I say, practice confidence to set yourself up for success.

FINDING YOUR
Passion

"Just follow your passion," is something that you often hear people say. You think to yourself that you'd love to do just that if only you knew what your passion was. You may be the type of person who works hard and gives things your all. You are committed to finishing tasks, and of course, goal-digging. When you know what you are getting into, nothing can stop you. But before you dive headfirst into being unstoppable, you have to first know what it is that you want to be unstoppable doing.

Some people just know what it is their heart beats for. We all have that friend or family member who has been doing the same thing for years. When you see them 'working' they are doing it with passion and zeal. Even when things get tough, you know, they can see beyond blocks in the road on to the win ahead. You may be just a little bit jealous that they seem to know exactly what they want out of life. They seem to have it all together. All of us aren't so lucky.

Have you ever asked yourself, "What am I passionate about?" If so, you are not alone. Many people float through their lives having no real idea of what they want out of life. Many follow the American Dream because they think that is just what they are supposed to do. That, or they live up to the image that they've overheard their parents talking about for years. The sad thing in both scenarios is you are living up to other people's expectations instead of your own. Drake coined the acronym YOLO, which stands for 'you only live once.' It's a younger, more way to say *carpe diem*, 'seize the day.' If you're not living for yourself, taking life by the horns and creating the life you want for yourself, what are you really doing?

Before figuring out how your passion can make you money, you have to know what that passion is. You have to make an effort to find out what that is. If I were to ask you what is bothering you, you would be specific: a demanding spouse, juggling overactive kids' schedules, petty co-workers, or stagnant sales from their dessert line. But if I asked you how to fix these things, your answers would be a lot more broad: happiness, making six-figures a year running my business, inner peace, or love. That's like going to a restaurant ordering something really good to eat and a beverage that will quench your thirst. Can you imagine how unsatisfying that meal would be leaving the total order up to chance without regard for your likes and dislikes or allergies? Just about as unsatisfying as your life leaving it in the hands of others.

This type of self-improvement takes effort, as I said before. Finding your passion won't come to you by sitting on your couch just thinking about it. Passion lives in your heart, not in your head. It's a feeling that rushes through you. It is an energy, an enthusiasm that commands attention.

Go Ahead, Find That Passion

Ok, so there are a few ways to realize what truly moves you completely; heart, body, mind, and soul. One awesome side-effect of actively finding your passion is that you will kind of lose bad habits along the way. With habits that weigh you down such as complaining, being stagnant, and procrastination pushed to the side, you will be able to move forward with more intention. Not only will you be more dedicated to setting and accomplishing goals, but you will do so without losing nearly as much time or energy.

> ➢ *Love everything you do.* From this point forward, you now have the realization that you can embrace what you have to do, or you can resist it. Either way, you still have to do it, right? So you might as well love it. Committing to loving your life and all that it encompasses helps to strengthen those "passion muscles." If you are trying to have an open mind enough to embrace loving everything that you do, you will see whether or not this is something you can really be passionate about.
>
> As creatures of habit, it is tough to think you could be whiny and complaining 75% of your day, then overly enthusiastic about the

remaining 25%. So if you approach everything with a great attitude, giving it a chance to grow on you and you still can't find that it makes your heart beat a little faster, that is not your passion. Many successful people have not let their circumstances lock them into a life they did not want. No matter what the situation was, they took responsibility for their experience within it, rather than being victims to circumstance. Loving what you do is the best way to get out of being born into a certain existence or failing your way into a life. If you can't change what you do, change how you do it.

➢ _Look for themes._ This is something we do unconsciously. You know how Netflix has that "suggested for you" category? They are able to suggest movies and shows based on those that you watch and/or rate. The concept is easy; yet, we don't take the time to see how we can suggest things for ourselves. Take a peek at the movies and shows you watch, the types of music you listen to, the things you do to wind down, and the activities that really get you excited. Do you see a pattern? If so, you are already spending your energy, time, and money on recurring themes in your life.

Use this knowledge to your advantage. Looking for something to light your fire could very well be right under your nose. Doing this you are thinking with your heart and body, not your mind. You can think yourself into or out of just about anything. Say you want to take salsa lessons. You think, "I really can't dance. It will be hard for me to learn that. Why would I do it? I would be so embarrassed." Yet every time you hear salsa music, your body moves to the beat. Why talk yourself out of it when you haven't given yourself a chance to explore it?

Is there anything that makes you light up when you talk about it? Like, you could literally talk about it for hours on end? Is there anything that you just can't get enough of? Keep in mind, passions don't have to "make sense" according to our upbringing or current circumstance. Shift your passion-seeking-attention to what is in your heart and how your body reacts. These are the things you should focus on.

➢ *Talk or teach.* Is there one topic in particular that you love to teach others or learn about yourself? If you aren't sure about this one, asking friends and family would be a good way to find out. They would be able to tell you what it is that you seem to always talk about wanting to do or wanting to learn.

➢ _Less talking, more doing._ This is where you take action steps to work on finding your passion daily. This requires little to no money. Beginners' classes can be free, or very inexpensive. Read articles, watch videos, write in your journal. As you get to know yourself, there will be themes that stick out to you as something you should dig a little deeper into. Find a way to participate in an activity that you love. If you truly love it, you will find a way.

Can Those Interests Make You Money

You should not be surprised if you find your passion hidden in something you do every day. If so, you can turn your passion into profit. Marc Anthony, Grammy-winning Latin heavyweight, also J. Lo.'s ex-husband got it right when he said, "If you do what you love, you'll never work a day in your life." Being passionate about doing or sharing something makes it easier to keep going when the going gets tough. And it will. Especially in entrepreneurship.

There is nothing new under the sun. Meaning of the 7.7 billion people on earth, someone is interested in what you have to say or will support what you produce. When I started iGoalDig, I did so knowing that as I encouraged myself to reach goals, launch businesses, and manage my family life, I could be doing the same for others who wanted to actually reach the goals that they set for themselves. I was passionate, not only about my message, but also to see people in my t-shirts, learning from my seminars, and asking me to help them find the formula to their success.

Incorporating your passion into an existing business or career is golden because the way has already been made, you just have to make it profitable. Many coaches will say that merging the two will lead to financial freedom, as well as free time. It also leads to a greater sense of fulfillment which will bring you more happiness in the end. Feelings of fulfillment and happiness are priceless.

Your creativity will determine how well you are turning your passion into a profit. Ask yourself these questions:

1. *Who's willing to pay for it?* Lisa Price, founder of the hair and skincare brand, Carol's Daughter launched her brand back in 1993 to answer the call of black women leaving relaxers to boast their natural hair to a lack of products. The "ethnic hair aisle" at most stores comprised of only a few shelves of sub-standard products that did not live up to the expectations of consumers. Inside of her apartment, she set up shop focused more on not blowing up her apartment than gaining customers. She was so

passionate about having hair care options to make her hair more manageable and presentable, that her brand grew into a household name as a multi-million dollar business. As a result, the brand was ultimately acquired by beauty powerhouse L'Oreal.

2. *Can your passion make a difference to others?* Joe Reynolds was a guy who loved adventure. In 2007, inspired by the popular TV show "The Amazing Race" he decided to create unique, fun events that everyone could enjoy. These events would encourage teams of people to discover their city through a series of clues leading to mental and physical challenges. In just five years, Red Frog Events, based out of Chicago, grew to employ 60 full-time employees, host events in 35 cities in the U.S. and three internationally, received over 600,000 participants and brought in a revenue of $85 million. He shared his passion for competing to create fun experiences for others to have that outlet as well.

3. *Have you mastered your craft?* Having knowledge and talent are not enough. Before you can start a passion-driven business, you must learn as much as you can. You must be willing to sharpen your skills, enhance your knowledge, and stay on top of fresh trends. In doing this, you will rise up as one to follow,

because you will become a trendsetter who creates new products/services that inspire others in your market. Remember, people don't see the work that goes into it, they just see the end result. They will see you as well-versed on the topic, having experience and know-how...or not.

4. *Do you know how to make money?* Don't laugh, this is a serious question. Many people just jump into launching a business without any idea what they are doing. They let their idea grow legs and run off without doing the research as to competitors in the market, market trends, consumer desires, or current branding. Eventually, the idea will run away from them causing them to close their business because they are so frustrated from losing money or simply not making any. Don't be this person. Commit yourself to financial education. "While passion is a key to attracting financial rewards, making more money also means learning to live below your means, asking for what you are worth, investing, and spending wisely," Valerie Burton says. Learn from leaders in your market and be dedicated to being financially savvy.

If you are able to fashion a life around something you love, you will not regret it. Don't miss out on the opportunity to hone in on skills that incite passion in you, while being profitable for you.

Everybody

IS DOING IT

And, what is *IT* exactly supposed to be? Growing up, "everybody is doing it" had a certain meaning. We would say it to our parents to convince them to let us do things like go to a party, wear make-up, or spend the night over a friend's house whose parents they didn't know very well. We thought by coming at them with a sort of peer pressure where their peers – the other parents – were letting their kids do *IT*, our parents should do the same for us. Our argument was so we could be in support of something, so we could be considered more a part of a group. Would there even be a need to use "peer" pressure if the activities were those that parents didn't want us to avoid?

Now, "everybody is doing it" has a much different meaning. It is a way to keep ourselves out of something; a way to hide behind getting something done. We try to show others that we want to go against the crowd showing some sense of individuality. Is it that or are we punking out? It seems that rather than chance failing in some way, especially where it's noticed by other people, we rather just not do *IT* at all.

Back in the day, I would have said, just because everybody is doing it doesn't mean you should – like jump off a bridge. Today I'm saying, just because everybody is doing it doesn't mean that you shouldn't or can't. Big difference.

First, we have to determine what *IT* is. Is *IT* doing something risqué like trying drugs or having an aggressive stock portfolio? Is *IT* trying a new diet fad that doctors seem to be on the fence about or getting a trainer and doing meal prep? You have to first look at the *IT* to determine if it's even worth going down the road to contemplate doing. If *IT* has to do with an activity or mindset that will challenge you to scale your business or level up your success, then yes, that is worth considering. If *IT* will push you to greatness, exploring a side of yourself that you never knew existed, let's go for it. The last thing you want to do is get stuck in a loop of doing the same thing…every day…for the next ten years. You will look up and wonder what happened to your life. Since you are reading *Diary of a Goal Digger*, I already know that is not you.

A few examples of goals that everybody else is going after that you should:

> ➢ Go back to school
> ➢ Starting a business

> ➤ Branding themselves on social media to gain a following
> ➤ Public speaking
> ➤ Writing a book

These are all *IT* things that seem to be more popular these days that you know you want and need to do, but are afraid you will far short of.

Now that we've determined that this *IT* is something that you really should be investing in, let's move forward.

Is Everybody Really Doing IT*?*

Chances are, they are *not*. You just may be letting fear over take you. Have others been doing it? Possibly. Are they doing it in increasing numbers? Also, very possible. One of the advantages of having social media is that you are potentially able to reach a worldwide audience. As a result, you are also in the worldwide audience that others want to reach. That being said, at the click of a button you are able to come into "contact" with countless businesses, entrepreneurs, and influencers. It is much easier to see what the world is up to now than it was, say 15 years ago.

The more people you see, the more you see what others are doing. Don't let this intimidate you. Are they really doing your *IT* or just talking about doing *IT*? It's one thing to set a goal for yourself and commit to making it happen. It's totally different to post about your goal and talk about it, but without putting action behind the words. Often times, that is what's happening. I was one of those people. I wanted to write a book. Talked about writing a book to my friends and family. Then the conversation spilled to my followers and social media family. Being a woman of my word, I knew I could not just continue to say I was writing a book without producing any results. I was embarrassed that someone was going to call me out on not living up to the hype I was giving myself.

There is a clear difference between those in the paint doing *IT*, and those ranting from the sidelines about doing *IT*.

Has What You're Doing Already Been Done?

Let's be clear, there is nothing new under the sun. Of course when you are sharing your ideas with someone, the last thing you want to hear is that your idea is not unique. You want to believe that you are the only person with that awesome idea or talent and you are also the only person who can execute the exact way you are thinking. Almost every idea has been implemented in some form or fashion. No matter what line of business you are in, there are others who are successful in it. They have already made names for themselves and have carved out their lane in it. That should not stop you from moving forward; particularly if you are a creative.

Before you talk yourself back out of *IT*, ask yourself, "What else would I rather be doing?" You cannot compare your idea phase to someone else's being-paid-to-public-speak-about-the-field phase, so if there isn't anything that you'd rather do, stick to it. That alone should get you out of comparing yourself to others and using them as inspiration instead. When you are doing what is in your heart to do, it does not matter that others are doing it, or appear to be doing it better. You can still get in there and make a difference. If you find that there is something else you'd rather spend time and energy on, change your path to head in that direction.

Acknowledge the market, but don't let it overwhelm you. If there is a sizable market, that means there is a demand for the product/service/idea that you have. This is a good thing. One of the reasons why it seems like everyone is doing what you are setting out to do is because that's where your focus is. If you are starting a graphic design company and you begin posting images you have created using certain hashtags and following other graphic designers, guess what? More graphic design companies are going to be showing up in your feed. You'll also see more ads for graphic design firms. Be aware of the market that is out there, but limit how much exposure you have to competitors as much as possible. It's easy to feel like everybody does it when you only follow others who do what you do.

Why bother?

Is this something you have asked yourself? I'm sure you have. I have too. This is one of the questions you ask when you are searching for a reason not to do something. Again, trying to talk yourself out of launching into a new phase of your life. When you see others doing what you do, it's natural to ask that question. What if Beyoncé asked herself, why bother? What if she thought Alicia Keys, Mary J. Blige, and Erykah Badu are already killin' *IT*? Enough said.

When I first began exploring my entrepreneurial journey, I literally considered everything and tried most of everything. The *IT* that I tried was also something that everyone was doing, selling hair. Although I started off when the hair extension industry was just building, I still took into perspective that everyone was doing it and how was I going to separate myself from the rest. The key to separating myself from others was "being myself," and selling who I genuinely was. My first year of selling hair, I grossed over $100k. That alone showed me that it doesn't matter if everyone else is doing it, I'M DOING IT and that's what matters. One thing I learned in my sales career is that people buy from people they like. So who cares if the other girl has a better website or cuter packaging, people are going to buy from who they want to buy from. Now don't get me wrong, you still want your brand to be presentable and stand out but the key essential is understanding that people are going to rock with who they like, no matter what.

How Do You Separate Yourself?

In other words, how do you make your voice heard in a crowded marketplace? The whole point of differentiating yourself is to navigate through the noise to appeal to a certain audience.

One of the worst feelings in the world is feeling like you are jumping into a rat race without any chance of winning. Winning for different people means different things. You have to first decide what is your why. Determining why you have set this goal for yourself will help you to understand how winning is defined by you.

Is winning...
- ...getting a certain number of followers?
- ...making a specific income each month?
- ...publishing a book?
- ...growing a community to call on?
- ...being a top influencer?
- ...creating a legacy for your children?

How will you win? Well, you have to separate yourself of course. Consider what you have already done in working towards your end goal. The very fact that you are striving to make a difference in your life puts you a few steps ahead of those who are being complacent with where they are. Rome wasn't built in a day, neither will that business or those abs. Your business or new lifestyle is going to come with growing pains that you have to be prepared for.

➢ *Use your personality.* No, the idea to go back to school is not a novel one, but you can use your personality to get a leg up. In this case, you'd go to your professor's office hours for additional help which could be beneficial during grade time. As a real estate agent, showcasing your personality in videos would help prospective clients feel more comfortable with you representing them. Stand out, be you, not a part of the crowd.

➢ *Let your passion shine through.* Each new client you get should get the same, enthusiastic version of you. If you are performing in an area of business that excites you to help meet a need for others, show them that you are excited. People will get a strong sense of who you are by the way you treat them. Don't let them get you wrong.

➢ *You control the end result.* Ultimately, whether you succeed or fail is up to you.

You determine how much time you dedicate. You determine how many events you attend. You are the one who has to put in the work. So, you are only as successful as you want to be. If you aren't seeing the results you want, switch up your approach.

➤ *Do your research.* When you get ready to drive to a place you've never been before, you prepare. You can use the maps app in your phone or ask a person who is familiar with the area. Still, you don't just hop in the car and hope to get there. Success requires a level of preparedness. Know where you want to go and how you plan to get there. This may also include learning more skills to make yourself more valuable.

One thing that grinds my gears is when people have these great ideas and don't want to do the proper research to get to where they are trying to go. Google is your best friend! Almost everything that I have learned, I literally did the proper research, networked with the right people and worked my wrist before I expected the easy route. Closed mouths don't get fed but hands out don't get respected.

> ➢ _What is your value proposition?_ People want to know that you have something to offer them that is unique. All fast food joints have chicken sandwiches, but there is only one Chik-Fil-A original chicken sandwich. Figure out what separates you from others by what you have to offer that they don't. Maybe you bundle your services differently, perhaps your packaging is fun and one-of-a-kind. Once you figure out your specific value proposition, translate it to your target demographic to encourage them to see the value in working with or supporting you.

If They Are Doing IT, So What?

Don't let the sound of others' success stifle you from trying to make your mark. Them making a name for themselves does not mean there isn't room for yours, but it leads to a comparison trap. You will start to compare what you offer or the idea you have with what others are doing. Use them for inspiration. Do you think McDonald's compares itself to Burger King? Absolutely. But does it keep McDonald's from coming up with new dishes and contests? Absolutely not. They both became – and remain – household names off of burgers and fries. That does not stop them from cultivating their consumer bases.

There is enough room for everyone to be great. Use what others are doing to separate yourself from them. It doesn't matter that there are one million companies that offer the same services as you. They aren't you, which means you can bring your own flavor to make it yours. Be optimistic enough to believe that your ingenuity will work in your favor.

If you spend more time honing your craft, learning new techniques, reading up on the issues that people needed solved, you will not have time to be worrying about comparing yourself to anybody else. When the comparison trap knocks on your door, get out of your head and get your hands busy working. Come up with new products, plan classes, find places to speak, look for events to network at, just busy yourself with being better and gaining more knowledge. Enhance your strengths, celebrate them and be proud of them. You don't have to brag about them to use them to your advantage.

At the same time, you don't have to tear others down to feel good about what you are doing. It is not uncommon for us to criticize others to make ourselves feel better. This is a destructive behavior that could lead to you creating an enemy where you could have had a friend in your industry. Believe it or not, people who hear what you say about others will look at you sideways wondering what type of person are you to feel the need to belittle others. It does not reflect well on you or the moves you are making. Support others and their success; it could lead to more success for you down the road.

Either way you look at it whether you are using comparison to do something others are doing or to keep from doing something others are doing, comparison is the thief of joy.

HAVING A JOB & BEING AN
Entrepreneur

We all know an entrepreneur who made the huge leap from being employed full-time to being a full-time entrepreneur. For some, it works like a charm; yet for others, there is unnecessary risk associated with this approach. Many people talk about starting a business while having a job. For some, the job is the very reason why they can't start their business. For others, like me, having the job offers financial security while starting the business.

As you know by now launching a business does not mean you have to quit your job altogether. It means dedicating an increasing amount of time and energy to a side hustle until you can live off of it full-time if that is what you desire to do.

For me, I had an amazing job as a salesperson for a Fortune 500 company. I had bills and responsibilities just like everybody else. So, when I decided to venture into something I was passionate about, quitting my job cold turkey did not make sense financially for me. I still had dreams of living life on my terms, having the flexibility of time and money to travel, start a family, and all that good stuff. Before getting to the vision of Chiara's life I saw in my head, I had to put one foot in front of the other, I had to start my business.

It wasn't hard to carve out time from my 9-to-5 to drive toward my goal of launching my tax business. Many successful companies began this way. Instagram founders Kevin Systrom and Mike Krieger worked nights and weekends on building their platform. Initially, the app was more like Foursquare, where users check-in to locations. They got very little traction and changed the setup to be all pictures. This is where their glow-up happened. By maintaining their day jobs, they were able to take their time, research their market, and play around with formats until they found one that worked.

Another advantage of this approach is you'll be less likely to take out loans. If you're anything like me, being in debt is not something I'm ok with. Maintaining your job means you have a steady income. As you are growing your business, you will be better able to ride the ebbs and flows of your business' financial successes and droughts. That, for many people, is the biggest stressor of having a business: financial worry.

Here are three questions I asked myself before starting my business

Is your job flexible enough to give you time to be an entrepreneur?

You're thinking if you really can't put your all into working a full-time job and trying to launch your hair boutique, it might not work. You don't want to get home at 7:00 and half-ass it. Where is the time going to come from with kids looking for dinner to be put on the table? Some jobs don't give you the flexibility to be an attentive parent due to the schedules and workloads. You may feel like you're already missing so much.

From my standpoint, it was easy for me to have a job while launching my business because I had a flexible job. As an inside salesperson, I didn't have to go into the office all of the time. Besides that, it wasn't a very stressful job either. There was no work to be taken home. My job stayed there. All of my clients were virtual and I handled them remotely, meaning there were no after-hour meetups or drives to talk to clients.

Sometimes jobs are so stressful, there is no room mentally to do anything else. Being an entrepreneur isn't easy, so if you're already stressed out at work and at home with whatever may be going on with your family, it may seem impossible to be attentive to a business. That is why some people automatically say, "I have to quit working to start my business." They already know with their current day-to-day life/work balance, they can't stretch themselves any thinner. So the smart ones plan ahead by saving at least 6 months of living expenses as not to have money worries on their mind on top of starting a business.

Flexibility is not just about time. Do you have the mental ability to run a business *and* work for a company *and* have a social life *and* manage your family? It has to all make sense. Running a business requires flexibility in more than just one realm.

I used my job as the perfect launching pad. My first tax clients were my co-workers. I knew they needed and could afford my services, and since we worked on a team together, they knew me as a person. Unlike many entrepreneurs who initially recruit family and friends as clients, I recruited my co-workers.

Do you cheat on your job with your own business?
I've done radio and blog interviews where I talk about starting my business as I "cheated" on my job. This is not to convince others not to work

while at work, but in all honesty half of the time I was at work, I was working on getting my business together as well. I would be researching things pertaining to my business, emailing people, taking calls and more. I was clocked in at work, waving at my business like, Hey girl heeeeey! I would leave for my lunch break to run to the post office so I could mail out hair orders. Instead of being 100% present, I probably spent close to half of the time I was clocked in tending to my own business. And if you can do that without it affecting your job, that is where balance comes in.

Some jobs are high demand, as I mentioned, so there is no flexibility to do anything while you're at work. If you have one of those jobs where you sit at the computer for several hours a day, and you can sneak in a few emails or research or planning, your business is like your side piece and the job is your main relationship.

Cheating on your job with a business or a side hustle is similar to cheating on your mate in the same aspect that you are giving both parts of you away to different entities. You are dividing your mental capacity, your energy and your physical ability. You care about them both enough to balance your time between them because you're trying not to give up either one just yet. Let's be honest, most people who work are doing so because they need their jobs. Even if they are running a good business, it's not enough to sustain the lifestyle that they want. Some people are ok with working a job and dabbling in business on the side the same way some people are comfortable with having a boyfriend or husband and a guy on the side. Physically, you're showing up to work each day yet, still working at vending events or running errands for your business, the same way some are physically involved with two people. Emotionally, you're invested in your job because there is the security of having that paycheck while operating your business is built on hopes and dreams. You don't want to neglect either of them, your job because you need it or your business because you want it. You're devoting your time to covering all bases on both of them.

Could the time you devote to your job make you more money if you used it toward your business?

I feel like it's obvious that if you weren't working your job, you could be fully focused on your business. If those 40 hours a week that are put into a job could be put into a business, of course the business would flourish. My thinking was, I'm spending 40 plus hours a week here at my job, if I put that same amount of time, energy, and skillset into my own business, I could make a 6-figure business for myself instead of making millions for this company. Even though it wasn't the same platform, my small business versus a company that had a household name after operating since 1983, I could make myself successful.

Think about going into a store and the employees are going so hard for McDonald's, they make you think they are a McDonald themselves, LOL! Even though employees like that annoy me when they follow me around the store or quickly get defensive with customers about the products offered in the store, I admire the passion I see in them. Imagine if they took that same passion and put into their own brand, how successful would their businesses be? Think about the videos on social media where you have workers who make $10-$12 an hour tackling thieves who steal from their stores or arguing and getting beat up, putting their life on the line for what? A regional manager, not even the business owner, who doesn't even know their name? Now think about translating that same energy into building a brand and how they could beast it out. I don't like it from a consumer side, but watching them from an entrepreneurial standpoint, I think, *Damn I would love for them to work for me going hard like that.* Getting $200 a week from a multi-billion dollar company.

Once you find that awesome business idea that you are passionate about, holding on to your job while working it won't feel like you're putting in two 40-hour work weeks even if you are. If you are flirting with the idea of having that business, then dive into that relationship while maintaining your job, your side hustle side piece could turn into your main before long.

BEING
Overwhelmed

When you become overwhelmed emotionally, it can consume you. Most of us will face an event that completely overtakes us at some point in our lives. It's something that is introduced into our worlds making it nearly impossible for us to manage. That thing for me was motherhood.

Becoming a mom completely changed everything about me. It changed the way I work and the way I approach things. Overwhelmed is the perfect word to describe how I felt. It slowed me down a lot to the point where I almost stopped working because it was so much. I did just enough to get by which was not this hustler's usual work ethic at all. My brain was not in work mode at all and this lasted for two years. Thank God I have a spouse who could accommodate to my transition without it causing an interrupt in my finances or lifestyle. Going through the transition of becoming a mom caused me to lose a quite a bit of my momentum.

Before having my daughter, I spent my entire days in work mode. All day, every day. My brain was always on, thinking about what was next to come. I hosted events, went to events, and if you know anything about Atlanta, you know there's no shortage of things to do here. My creativity was on full blast 24/7. I'd recently launched iGoalDig and promoting women's empowerment through the events I hosted or was a part of. iGoalDig had become a movement in itself. I branded with t-shirts that were quickly becoming a hot commodity, putting on seminars under that name, and speaking on panels about entrepreneurship. I had even begun interviewing other entrepreneurs for iGoalDig TV to get a different perspective for followers and fans who supported the movement. Things were really taking off! Even while pregnant, I was keeping that positive momentum flowing by keeping up with the demand in my tax business. As brand visibility increased, so too did blog inquiries and people reaching out to me.

As you may or may not know, "pregnancy brain" is one of the hallmarks of pregnancy. Many women complain of the pregnancy-induced brain fog that leads to forgetfulness and short-term memory loss. I was no different. Things were starting to come undone and I was working hard to keep it all together.

In my mind, I thought I was doing a good job of staying on top of things. What I found out instead was that I was slowly becoming behind on where I felt like I needed to be. I was still able to maintain my tax business, but that was about it. I could not keep up with the work-life aesthetic I had going on.

Becoming a mom isn't easy at all, especially being a first-time mom. I was running a few businesses already; but, I did not think having my daughter would change me the way it did. Beyond becoming a mom, I was a stay-at-home mom. So whatever little work I was doing had to be nestled in between her naps, feedings, bath times, and full alertness of learning and exploring her world. I thought the stay-at-home mom's life was going to be cool. I figured I'd be able to easily balance work life and mom life since I could do it all, for the most part, from the comfort of my own home. For me, entering this new phase of my life was anything but easy. It almost started to seem like it was practically impossible. My baby encompassed my world which I couldn't complain but I knew I needed to strategize things differently to keep things going as well as they were before.

Everything came to a screeching halt. I didn't know it happened, until it happened. I literally woke up one day was said, "Damn...ok." It had all changed. In all honesty, even though I began ramping my work game back up when she was around one years old, it still took time for me to get close to what I consider normal. Once I realized that I needed to go super hard, harder than ever, it made me feel like I would never gain that traction ever again. And if I did, it would take a lot of effort.

I can't lie, I became frustrated wondering how I let myself get off the ball. I watched others around me and on social media who had been in my workshops or clients who I'd helped start their businesses and they were taking off. Looking at myself, I was still around, but not making forward progress. It was strange for me to be in a place where I didn't have anything new going on. It was also a complete setback to me to be in a race where it felt like others, who I had been running with, were surpassing me. To get myself back into it, I dibbled a little bit here and there with relaunches and campaigns, but it wasn't the same. I relaunched iGoalDig, then stopped putting in the effort needed to sustain what the plan was. I wasn't ready to come back, I was just putting something in motion because I felt like I should.

I know I'm not alone. I feel like many women go through feelings of being overwhelmed. And not necessarily about becoming a mom. Feeling crushed under the weight of a different circumstance can happen because of the loss of a loved one, a relationship ending, losing a job, or gaining new responsibilities. Anything causing a change in your life that alters who you are is what being overwhelmed means.

If you are overwhelmed, it shouldn't be that hard to pinpoint what sets you off. However, it could be a combination of things because going day-to-day, stressors can become a challenge to manage. A traumatic experience could have come out of nowhere or work can be driving you up a wall leading into a months' long process of losing yourself. Unfortunately, you may be on the receiving end of a series of events, one after another, in a short amount of time.

A few things that can lead to feeling overwhelmed are...

- ➢ Financial insecurity

- ➢ Relationship issues

- ➢ Mental or physical health issues

- ➢ Death of a loved one

> ➢ Suffering mental, physical, or sexual abuse

> ➢ Habitual lack of sleep

> ➢ Poor nutrition

> ➢ Parenthood

Being overwhelmed can lead to depression if you're not careful. Anger, anxiety, irritability, poor life management, and lack of motivation are key symptoms of feeling like life is just too much. Some who suffer from not being able to handle the swift transitions may experience shortness of breath, chest pains, uncontrollable crying, and panic attacks. Pinpointing what is bringing you to feel these symptoms is crucial in knowing how to make it right.

Ask For Help

Like just about any self-respecting mom, I take on everything. Not that we try, but that's kind of just the way things end up working out. I had to do something that was out of my character…spread out the responsibilities. Of course I'm not saying that her dad did not help me around the house or take care of her. I needed him to take on a bigger role. I had to get out of the mindset of, *Let me do everything, I'll figure it out.* Yeah, I was that girl. It wasn't working out for me. It was ok in the sense that things were getting done the way I wanted them done. The caveat was that it was hindering me in life because I wasn't allowing my support system to work. I had to talk myself into letting my man help out, letting my mom help out, and utilize the resources I had to help me get back to myself. Not the different version of myself I saw in the mirror every day, because I felt like I no longer looked like me, but the Goal Digging Chiara I knew I was.

Nothing Wrong With Being A Little Selfish

I handled being overwhelmed by being a little selfish. As a people pleaser, I want to make sure everybody around me is good. I decided that I would replace my entrepreneurial ventures with motherhood instead of adding another hand to juggle everything. My focus was on being a good mother and a good spouse. I threw my wants and needs to the side for the sake of my family. I wanted to make sure my man was a happy person and my daughter was happy as well. I forgot that I was just as important as they were. I recognized that I had to find a way not to take away from them, but to give to myself as well. I had to flip the script, giving back to myself to re-energize my spirit. I planned and booked a solo trip, then I invested in a real estate class, which is something I'd really wanted to do. I put my daughter in daycare, not only to give her peer social interaction but also to give me a much-needed break.

The word "selfish" has such a negative connotation; however, I was able to give the word a positive meaning. There is a good side of being selfish, where you take care of yourself to be the best version of yourself. To show up grounded and more healthy, setting aside time for you is the best way to do it. Selfishness is more in our nature because instinct urges you to survive. You have to sleep. You have to have food and water. You must have shelter. These are a few examples of necessary and healthy selfishness. As we continue through life, going to school, being around siblings or other kids in our family, we are taught to be considerate of others. As nurturers, women naturally want to make sure that everybody under our roof is good. To a fault.

Michelle Obama told Barbara Walters in a 20/20 interview in 2011, "One of the things that I want to model for my girls is investing in themselves as much as they invest in others." She went on to illustrate this idea using a plane analogy. You know how they teach you to put your oxygen mask on in an emergency before helping the person next to you? Same thing, in this way, turning attention to yourself first will help you to be more generous towards others.

What are positive reasons goal diggers should be more selfish?

➤ *Better health*...Selfish people take time out for themselves. This means they schedule exercise and vacations which go a long way to impact physical and mental health. They work hard, while also believing they deserve to have much-needed rest. And they don't feel bad about it.

➤ *You'll be a better leader*...Confidence is a trait of selfish people. Because they are confident in themselves, they are less likely to give up reaching goals. They also are not afraid to ask for raises and promotions.

➤ *Happiness is around the corner*...You will know who you are, what you like, and be able to communicate that to others. You will know how to set boundaries for yourself and others that illustrate what you are and are not willing to do.

Connect With The New You

So you are out living your best life then SKURRRRRRRT! That thing comes out of nowhere and forces you into a patch that you can't navigate. You think you can handle it; but you can't. Your life has completely changed in a sense, and you have to try to regain the traction you had. It can seem impossible for some, tough for others, while some never skip more than one beat.

I spoke to a few moms around me to see how they grasped having kids and still keeping up with life. Some of the women kinda shrugged and said, "Well, I'm done with that life," of chasing their dreams to be larger than life. They chose instead to settle into really enjoying what motherhood had to offer them. They wanted a more normal life-changing their definition of success to being a good mother. Others decided to take it slow and get back to a working pace when they felt they were ready.

Be patient with yourself. Realize that the new you will not emerge overnight. It may be difficult for you to ask for help or tell others no. You may also feel a little guilty for just running away from your responsibilities for a while. Understand that changing anything is a process, but your sanity and ability to move forward is so much worth the wait.

Networking

Networking can seem like such a naughty word because some people 'hate' to network. They cringe at just the thought of it, feeling a dash of apprehension before going into a social or professional setting with the goal of networking. As soon as you read the word, an image instantly popped into your head. It may have been a networking event you went to recently or one from the days of your networking past. Either way, we've all had our fair share of networking.

Let's think about the typical networking event setup. You go to a place you've probably never been before, a stuffy hotel ballroom situation or a restaurant and you drag a friend or co-worker along with you. You walk in there intending to shake x amount of hands or pass out x amount of business cards. You try to do just that. But it's weird, right? In the quick time you are there, you are only able to make quick, surface-level interactions. You are forcing yourself to engage them for the sole purpose of exchanging information.

"Hi! I'm Sarah, what do you do?" can seem like a brash way to begin a conversation. Yet, that's exactly how many interactions at networking events begin. Now, of course, it is appropriate to ask what someone does for a living because after all, you need this information to determine whether or not you and this person can be assets to each other.

"Here's my card," is the way so many of these conversations end. Even though you know their business card will end up in your business card oblivion, you are always hopeful that yours will somehow remain at the top of their pile and they will remember who you are, can connect your face to your name and keep in contact with you. Personally, I can't remember a time I ever contacted someone based on a two-minute conversation and a card exchange. Or better yet, being out in the world and having someone walk up and say, "I'm a hairstylist, here's my card," and walk away.

Let me be clear. It's almost impossible to succeed in business without networking. How can you run a business without having outside connections? On a social level, we network without even thinking about it with our hair stylists, nail techs, mechanics, and where we shop. Believe it or not, when we choose a neighborhood grocery store, even that is a form of networking because we are deciding to patronize that business. We naturally network as we move in our day-to-day lives because we are moving with a purpose. Trying a new restaurant and deciding to go back because you liked the food and ambiance is networking. It's the same as meeting someone, having a connection with them and finding commonalities. The day-to-day type of networking is less forced since you're doing it on an everyday basis.

What if you created purposes and strategies for business and career networking? Do you think networking events would be more fruitful? They were for me. After changing my approach to 'networking,' I found that I was more comfortable with it all. I realized that there were other ways to forge meaningful relationships than bouncing from one networking event to the next.

Less… "Hey, here's my card."
More… Building genuine relationships.
The skill of networking goes beyond the numbers game of meeting as many people as possible and passing out as many cards as you could carry into the event. One quality connection is much better than 15 super quick, casual ones. Don't just skate

on the surface of superficiality, focus on having one or two deep, meaningful conversations. You want to listen to their goals and interests responding with your view on those you have in common. Keep in mind that networking can lead to lifelong relationships. Don't shy away from extending an invitation to the person sitting next to you at a conference to join you for lunch, or extend an offer to get together for drinks to a person you really gelled with at a small party.

Less... Me, me, me
More... What do I have to offer?
You should focus more on what you have to offer, instead of thinking solely about what you want. Instead of walking into a room with a list of wants such as a specific number of cards to collect or flyers to pass out, reverse your aim. Make a list of what you can offer to those who you meet so when they tell you what they do, you can chime in with a 'special offer' of 20% off their first service booked with you, or a free e-book on your website that you will email them. You want to give them a reason to follow-up with you. Another clever way of getting to know them is by asking, "What projects are you working on right now?" More than likely, instead of focusing on their 9-to-5 projects, they will jump

into a pleasure project. This helps you create another level of connection as you get to know more about who they are as a person. If they are working on something you don't have knowledge of, offer to connect them with someone in your network who does.

Less... Elevator pitch
More... Authenticity

So, you know that brief, persuasive speech you give for people to take an interest in your business, brand, or cause? That is an elevator pitch. The term was derived from only having a quick 20-to-30 seconds, or an elevator ride, to capture someone's interest. But with elevator pitches, it seems they can feel even more unnatural because you aren't catering who you are and what you have to offer to your audience. Elevator pitches are general, salesy even. You can cultivate more authentic connections by catering your 'elevator pitch' to the person you are talking to. Rather than approach with a cookie-cutter pitch, wait until after a few exchanges in the conversation to find a common ground to introduce them to your service or product. Being salesy or pushy is a complete turnoff; you're shooting out before you even start. This is a dated gimmick that everyone knows about and will quickly write you off for. At the end of the day, you can't sell a relationship. You can sell your product by showcasing the benefits of it or how it can solve a problem in their life, but relationships are earned.

Less... Awkward networking events
More... Social media millennial gold

Perhaps networking events aren't your thing because you are too shy. There are varying levels of terror tied to being in an environment swarming with scary strangers. We may go through the motions of showing up and being active while there, but usually the result is not worth the agony we suffered while being there. The beauty of the internet is that you can easily connect with so many people. People you know, but also those who you don't. Social media has clever ways of letting you see how many connections you and a 'stranger' have in common. You get a peek at the type of person they are, as well as their likes and dislikes before you send the first DM or inbox message. Maybe you aren't shy, but you still don't appreciate the feeling of being trapped in a stranger's face trying to coax a conversation between you two. You'd rather connect and stay in touch without being overbearing. For me, that is the case. I'd rather not sit and hold idle chit chat when we are both busy people who value our time and it could be better spent somewhere else. Don't miss an opportunity to connect through comments or private messages.

Less... Traditional networking
More... Creative thinking

You don't have to go to a networking event or ask a friend to introduce you anymore. The latter still works, because then your friend could speak on your behalf. However, if you get creative with the way that you show support, you are still networking. For example, a poet you know has a new book coming out and you want to show support. Separate yourself from the crowd by not just commenting on their post, but reposting it and adding a genuine caption...with a tag to the author! They are much more likely to recall that gesture than just a comment or emoji. If someone you've seen is hosting an event or give-back to the community, reach out and ask how you could help. Again, doing things that others seem to be too busy to do or don't want to be bothered with will set you apart from the pack. Showing support is a huge way to network. It goes a very long way! I have internet friends who are really internet friends. We established a bond somewhere along the way and are involved in each other's lives. We are watching each other's children grow up, celebrating milestones, seeing businesses launch, and we are genuinely happy for progress being made, while also saying a prayer when needed. This is networking, the millennial way.

Networking can work for you if you rethink the negative connotation. It can be fun, more authentic, less salesy, and still be results-driven. Give it another chance using some of these tips. Now ask yourself, how will I intentionally network differently?

TUNNEL
Vision

When you think about what you want to do in life and business, your mind can be filled with ideas. Even though these ideas may all be related, you could still come up with several different ideas. What do I mean by that? Let's think about it. Say you want to start something that you can call your own, so you brainstorm. At the end of brainstorming, you may have come up with the following possibilities:

1. Handmade bath and body care company
2. Social media marketing
3. The importance of self-care
4. Shea butter based products
5. A non-profit organization to help teen girls get personal hygiene items
6. Become a public speaker
7. Open your own brick and mortar

Notice these items are all somewhat similar and can be under the same umbrella, but the focus of each is somewhat different. There is a combination of entrepreneurship and change of lifestyle. This is where tunnel vision narrows the focus and #igoaldig is brought to life. We hear the term "tunnel vision" used all the time, but humor me while I will define what tunnel vision is. Tunnel vision is having a long-term view of something, knowing what you want and honing in on that thing. Before you set out to accomplish any goals, you have to know *what* it is you want to do and *why* it is you want to do it.

One of the most important keys to success, business or personal, is getting focused and staying focused. As a small business owner, especially starting out, it's more about the launch than anything else. On the personal side, the result of tasting the win is what it's all about. You have so many awesome ideas of how to improve your life and you are finally able to narrow it down to the one you want to work toward, you do your research and get your plan or funding in order. Along the way, you have stars in your eyes about being the next Oprah or Beyoncé because you just know your business is not like any of the other 627,000 new businesses that open each year (according to SBA estimates) and your goal of purchasing your first home or obtaining your college degree is going to put you over the moon. Once you reach this milestone, you are sure doors will open for you and your self-esteem will definitely grow. You see yourself being able to ante your lifestyle, proudly boasting to the world what you've accomplished. To make it even more enticing, you have even already written the social media post in your mind.

After you get started and see how much effort and grit go into not only taking the first steps, but maintaining momentum, you easily get discouraged. You become disgruntled with your idea as you watch your dream of being bossed up slowly fade into a distant, watercolor memory. Frustrated because you want to live the dream, you develop lifestyle attention deficit disorder (ADD). You jump ship, giving up on your goal before you really had a chance to succeed.

STOP!

It can be quite easy to move on to the next, seemingly promising, idea. Especially since ideas are so promising in our heads. Tunnel vision doesn't get the accolades it deserves. Traits like hard work, dedication, strong work ethic, #teamnosleep, grind, and motivation are often heard in the same sentence as entrepreneurship and goal-digging. Tunnel vision plays a significant role in your ability to be productive and successful. Being focused means your goals and objectives are clear. At any time you are faced with a decision, you pit the outcome against how it will affect your goals and objectives. Decisions are based on making progress towards your goals and objectives. The alternative to having tunnel vision is, well, having lifestyle ADD. You are jumping from idea to idea, not really staying with anything long enough to make headway with any of them.

Why Focus Matters

Big wins are conceived, constructed, and developed by entrepreneurs who tunneled in on the progress of their dream every single day. It is no accident that people who constantly achieve success again and again are those who know how to block out noise from the rest of the world. Having tunnel vision allows you to think and act in a way that moves you forward. Think about it from a business standpoint, Pizza Hut's focus is pizza. Sure they have other things on the menu such as salads, chicken wings, and desserts, but their advertising is all about pizza. Firestone repairs cars; you can get your oil changed, new tires, or your A/C fixed. What you can't do is go to Pizza Hut for car repair. Customers aren't confused because the branding has been consistent.

Difficulty With Tunnel Vision

Lack of focus is not all your fault. In 2019, we have so much technology vying for the attention of our fingertips, it is easy to become bombarded with shiny, new glimmers to take away your attention. Searching the web and social media are all within a second's reach on the phones that we can't live without and the smart TVs that we have in every room. We are bombarded with programming and competition – both distractions from you getting ahead. Some may argue that seeing how others are doing it is wise, and it is. However, if you become obsessed with watching others just to compare their 'successes' with your losses, that is a distraction.

All distractions are not bad. Some distractions keep us feeling excited to be interrupted by like: children, family, friends, jobs, spouse/partner, exercise, being healthy, household chores. Ok, the last item, household chores may have taken it a bit too far, but you get the point. Everything that takes time away from you working toward your goal and the tunnel vision that you are trying to cultivate can't possibly be bad. These things have their place – and time – in your life.

The trick for you is to learn how to balance them so you are still able to put your most productive foot forward. The work-life balance thing can be a challenge, especially when you are doing more than just day-to-day living. Devoting a lot of time to one specific thing means something else will suffer. Ultimately, if you are not focused, your distractions may cause you to give up. You can be distracted by the idea of failure. Not being confident you can get that cosmetology degree could lead you not to study or do the required number of practice hours, which in the end will prevent you from getting it. Not being confident in yourself and your abilities will show in little things along the way that will have a big impact on what you're doing.

Do You Give Up Easily

I don't necessarily give up easily. I am a fighter. I fight people, I fight goals, I fight to the very end. I'm very strong-willed as being a Leo claims me to be. Ask yourself, *Does failing once make me give up?* There's a saying that one failure should not keep you from success. Personally, I feel that each 'no' puts you one step closer to a 'yes.' Think of failures as life lessons. When you fail, you learn. If and when those types of incidents happen again, you will know how to address them and move forward quickly without missing a beat. Also, you'll know how to direct others on the paths they can take to avoid missteps all together.

Many people approach goals like success is a straight path...you either get it right the first time, or it's not for you. That can't be further from the truth. "I started my online boutique, nobody bought any clothes from me. I'm done." That is not the mind of a goal digger. You should be eager to get back to the drawing board to see why no one bought clothes from you, what you can do differently moving forward, what can you add or remove from your offerings to make your boutique more enticing. If in your reflection, you see that you only posted once a week and no one responded to your sales, then you know your marketing needs more attention.

No matter what type of failure you have, look at the situation, identify what you think caused it, and fix it. Don't move forward in anger or frustration saying, "This just isn't for me." Move forward in growth. There is a difference between giving up and deciding now is just not the time to move forward with that goal. If you have a goal to buy a new car, but you're already struggling to pay bills each month, it's ok to decide buying a new car is not the way for you to be going at the time.

Tunnel Vision Has Benefits

Aside from what we've already discussed, having tunnel vision does have real benefits that will continue to show themselves in your life.

> ➢ *Speed...you will be quicker.* When your vision is aimed toward a specific goal, swerving away from distractions, your mind learns how to hone in on one task and that one task alone. So let's say you want to deliver a week's worth of social media posts for your business. Eliminating the obvious distractions like the TV and phone, and granting yourself a certain amount of time will create an environment for you to do just that.

We forget how amazing our minds are. We are limitless in reaching our creative and powerful potential. Imagine how quickly we could get tasks done when we tunnel in on   just one thing? If you tell yourself, I'm going to take the next two hours to write all of my social media posts for the next week and you actually give yourself the time and space to do it, you will do it. When the task is complete, you can go on to the next.

> *Your productivity will be of a higher caliber.* Giving a task 100% of your attention, you are able to get it done in less time and with fewer mistakes. The tunnel vision helps you to be more creative because you're so focused. You'll be able to solve more problems and see the picture ahead of you with more clarity. This really comes into play if you are easily distracted. When you can zone into your craft whether it be writing, playing music, graphic design, or photography, the results will show in your work.

> *Stress will back off.* The anticipation of a goal is very stressful, just about anyone will second that motion. But, when you know where you're going, you don't worry so much. Giving time and energy to distractions adds to stress. This isn't only saying when you stop completely working toward the goal, but having minor detours as well. Any pause or break in your flow can slow down forward movement. Sometimes,

that can be very hard to recapture. You may be stuck thinking, *Now, how do I get back on the right track again?* Trying to regain that focus causes you to stress out about the possibility of not plowing forward as consistently as you were before.

Identify What Drives You To Stay Motivated

One of the first things you should focus on is your 'why.'

Why did you start this business?

What do you have to gain?

What problem are you looking to solve?

Am I in this to make a better life for myself and my family?

Do I want greater visibility among my co-workers?

What are my priorities?

Being a mother is always a motivator. Having bills attack you every 30 days in your mailbox or inbox keep you motivated. If you have an inspiration to live a certain lifestyle such as taking trips, putting your kids in private school or buying expensive shoes, that will keep you motivated. But keep in mind. Everything is not about money. You could be working now to build a legacy of real estate so that when you pass away, your children will inherit those properties for passive income. Clearly identifying your driving force will help to keep that person or thing in the forefront of your mind so you don't let them down. If you don't know who or what you are doing it for, you will lose focus. But writing down your motivator will deter you from giving up so easily because you will feel like you are letting them down.

Getting Familiar With Affirmations

Recently, I asked someone if they practiced affirmations. They asked me what I meant. I found it hard to believe that in this day and age, someone did not even know what an affirmation was. I look at affirmations as confirming things within yourself.

I am a boss.

I am confident.

I am strong.

These are ways of confirming within yourself who you are, what you are, and who you want to be, then manifesting them. If you ever watched BET's *Being Mary Jane*, you will recall that she had sticky notes on her bathroom mirror. They were filled with affirmations. It is a good practice to put them up anywhere...in your car, on your screensaver, on your computer.   Constantly seeing them will remind you to bring these thoughts into your heart and mind.

I love how my cousin brought affirmations into her daily life. For years, as she drove her son to school every day, they practiced saying affirmations. *I am a man. I am strong. I am respectful.* The affirmations may have changed from day-to-day, but the act of saying them was the same. She started this back when he was in elementary and he just graduated high school. He's grown up to be such a good young man, everything she wanted him to be because of the positive affirmations and good parenting.

Saying affirmations is speaking these truths into the universe. If you wake up every day and say, "I am successful. I am rich. I am happy. I am a great mom," these things will manifest. You will be successful, you will be rich, you will be happy, and you will be a great mom. Just as you can speak positives into your life, you can also speak the opposite. "Girl, I'm broke. I can't afford to get that." You'll never hear me speak that way. Even if I'm low on funds and don't have any flexibility in my budget, I won't speak that over my life.

Use affirmations to help you stay focused on what you want and the type of life you want to have.

Tips To Staying Focused

Keeping your vision straight ahead on your goal is easier than you think. Here are a few simple tips:

Give yourself time-sensitive goals. Let's say you are looking to open up a boutique. Map out your goal for opening the boutique in increments of time. You may opt to go month-to-month as month one, month two, month three, or three months, six months, nine months, a year. Putting a timeframe on what you need to accomplish helps you remain focused. If in the first three months you assign yourself to find wholesalers, don't start designing a logo and working on a website too. You should be tunneled in on finding wholesalers, setting up accounts with them, and getting samples.

When you wear many hats, your time-sensitive goals should be in smaller chunks of time. For example, yesterday I was working on a client's taxes when a credit repair client texted me. What did I do? Immediately stop working on the taxes to hop online to check the files my credit repair client needed. Just that quick, with the ding of my phone, I halted my productivity. Remembering that for me to maximize my time and efficiency with the many hats I wear, I took a deep breath and stopped. I gave myself 60 minutes to dedicate to completing the tax client's file before I stopped to work on anything else. And it worked!

Have a dedicated workspace. Having cluttered rooms or desks is the norm. If you have 15 projects sprawled out everywhere all begging for your attention when working, it is hard to finish the task at hand without already having your mind on the next thing. Clean up your workspace. Make your workspace more inviting and less haunting, by getting rid of clutter. Organize things neatly so they are easy to find once you get ready to work on them.

Boss over your technology. Phones have silencers for a reason; TVs have off buttons. If you are a mother like me, I know that ringer isn't going to be turned off because anything can happen while your little ones are away at school. Texts and emails don't need audible alerts; social media updates don't need to pop-up on your phone. Or, you could simply turn your phone face down so you won't see them until you are ready. Learn how to disconnect, then reward yourself with five to ten minutes of scrolling to reinvigorate yourself before jumping into the next task.

Move forward in your productivity by getting your tunnel vision in check. You got this!

NOT
Giving Up

We've already established that beginning something new is exciting. Before you even get started, you'll be overcome by all sorts of emotions. Fear, frustration, lack of self-confidence will show their heads just a little bit initially. Then once it becomes time to put your plan into action, those three will become imminent dark forces, ready to take you out.

Regardless of what your goal is and how bad you want it, the temptation to quit is only one thought away. You will reach a point where your motivation hits a wall and you'll be challenged to keep it moving.

"Giving up is not an option!" people say. But the truth is when it comes to not giving up, that can be very hard. More often than not, when we set goals, we are going to be doing or learning something we know nothing about. The anxiety that brings with it can be paralyzing and for some, it freezes them right on out of their dreams. They would rather not make a move than go at the fear of uncertainty head-on. *What if I fail?* You may, but what if you succeed? Instead of looking at the pessimistic side of the coin, you should focus more on the possibilities.

Part of not giving up is maintaining the momentum that you have by finding the time to dedicate to your goal. Nelson Mandela said, "It always seems impossible until it's done." Guess what? It won't get done if you give up. Not only will you be letting your present self down, but also the awesome future self. See, when you are working toward a worthwhile goal, giving up could mean throwing away something wonderful. If you just stick to it, achieving the goal could be better than you thought it could be. It can lead to other, even greater opportunities.

#goaldigging is not just about setting a goal, making a plan, and achieving that goal. It is also about the transformation that takes place, who you will become. Think about a little girl learning to ride their bike for the first time. Initially, she's all excited about getting her new bike; she can't wait to ride it. She goes outside so her dad can teach her. Knowing she had a handle on riding with the training wheels, she's not thinking about the difficulty that awaits her without that aid. Smiling from ear-to-ear, she hops on the bike and her dad, who is holding on to the handlebars and the seat walks alongside her trying to make sure she has her balance. Dad lets go, she falls down. It's a shock to her and she cries, but she's not deterred. Dad holds the bike for her to get back on and when she does, he walks beside her guiding again, checking for her to have balance, then let's go. She falls down again. This cycle is repeated over and over.

For some children, after falling a few times they've had enough of eating the pavement. They don't want to learn or hurt themselves to the point where pedaling becomes a real struggle. Never before did she look at the grass, the driveway, or the mailbox as obstacles to get past. Now, those same things are causing her to fall. Her dad will continue to encourage her to stick with it, as will her other cheerleaders, friends, and family who are all outside watching and playing. After many tries, and many falls, she gets it and has learned to ride her bike.

Now, think about the transformation that has taken place in just that short stint of time. She's learned that if she is dedicated, she can accomplish what she sets her mind to. She's learned that she does have support, even when it seems like odds are stacked against her. She's also learned the everyday occurrences that she's normally oblivious to can become obstacles to overcome. But, with a bit of time and effort, she can overcome or steer around them.

For us, the transformation is the same. Whether your goal can be accomplished in a matter of hours or requires several months, if you don't give up, you can make it. Not only will you learn lessons in resilience as you go, but you will also be able to pass those lessons on to your children and those around you when they stand while giving up.

Does Failing Make You Feel Like Giving Up?

Back in 2008, Hillary Rodham Clinton was a junior United States Senator from New York who announced that she wanted to run for president. She campaigned her heart out, but did not even secure the Democratic Nomination. Many counted this as a failure. What would you have done? If the world knew you were gunning for a goal as unprecedented as being the first female President of the United States, and you couldn't even get your party to come together for you, how would you have handled this failure? You may have just given up, or said you would wait until the next opportunity to run again. Instead, she got herself one step closer to the White House by taking a position as Secretary of State. Hillary used her failure as a stepping stone; she didn't treat it like a cause to give up her political dreams.

By only focusing on the end goal, you are missing out on the benefit of the journey. It's not only important that you are making progress toward the finish line, but that you are growing as a person along the way. There is a reason you have this goal. Whether divinely directed or selfishly appointed, there is fulfillment in your purpose on the road ahead. You can be headed straight for your goal and when hit with a wall, life serves you the real reason you are on that path; it gives you a new mission. Your life is not meaningless, even if you haven't discovered what that meaning is quite yet. There will be people you can help, people you can lead, others who you will encourage, and a tremendous amount of inner personal growth for you.

If failing makes you feel like giving up, tell one of your accountability partners of your plan. I guarantee you they will give you a thousand reasons why you should keep going, or they will ask what the issue is and try to help you solve it. Remember, we are all connected. When you give up, you are not just giving up on yourself and your dreams, you are also dreaming of killing a bit for the ones who are rooting for you.

Watch Someone Else Persevere

Aside from the bucket of tears that will be shed, there is a lot to learn from the movie *Pursuit of Happyness*. It is inspired by the true story of Chris Gardner, a single father with a 5-year-old son who rises from homelessness to Wall Street legend. There are countless movies about seeing someone persevere against seemingly insurmountable odds but refused to quit. Yes, these types of movies will be emotional, but that may be just what you need to keep going. Nine times out of ten, your mountain will seem like a molehill when compared to Chris Gardner's, or Tyler Perry's who was homeless, yet still determined to bring his craft to the masses.

When you feel like quitting, watch an inspirational movie. Watching the character go through numerous trials will hopefully help you to follow suit. Go back to your *how*. Refusing not to give up does not mean you go back to attacking with the exact same POA (plan of action). Maybe the issue is with your method of attack. Have you ever heard the saying, "the definition of insanity is doing the same thing over and over and expecting a different result?" This is true. How can you continue to try something over and over, yet seek to see something different? If you feel like you have hit a brick wall, try a different route. Continue trying a different approach or strategy until you find one that gives you a desire that you are satisfied with. The result may not be perfect, but if it can get you over the hump so that you can continue on, roll with it.

Revisit Your Why

You set a goal because it has meaning behind it, you don't just pick a goal out of thin air. An important step to setting a goal is to have a reason "why" this goal is important to you. If your "why" isn't strong enough, it will be a challenge to remain motivate when adversity strikes. Before you begin #goaldigging, write out all of the reasons why achieving this goal is so important to you. If you don't think this list of "whys" will be strong enough to help keep you from giving up, find another goal. That means you don't want it bad enough or for the right reasons. The greater and stronger your reasons, the less likely you are to give up.

Affirmations

Positive affirmations are short statements designed to help you overcome self-sabotaging thoughts and behaviors. Though you may have heard of them, if you haven't tried saying them, it can be awkward. As discussed in Tunnel Vision, reinforce self-esteem, motivate positive self-talk, and subconsciously lead to better feelings. They help you create abundance in your life because they remind you of the life you want to have. By keeping these short phrases at the forefront of your mind, and repeating them, you are *affirming* what you believe about yourself.

Achieving your goals is far from easy. With the right mindset, attitude, and tenacity, you can and will do just that.

MAINTAINING YOUR
Momentum

You look around at your life and something needs to change, so you make a commitment to yourself to start something new. You set a goal of going to the gym, starting a business, getting serious about a new job search, or saving money. You have an end goal in mind, but getting started is the hard part, or so you think. In some ways, beginning this new journey brings an excitement that has you buzzing with what you're going to do once you reach this goal. Once you've mustered the strength to get started following your plan and a little time has passed, you realize that staying the course, not getting started is the hard part.

Seeing a new goal on your to-do list is not enough to keep you from flaming out. As time passes by, your energy levels concerning this new goal dwindle. It becomes less and less of a priority as it slips further down the list. Maintaining momentum toward the finish line while following your plan seems like one of the hardest things in life to do. However, Maintaining momentum toward the finish line while following your plan is a necessary thing you must do. Creating momentum requires increasing activities and thoughts that propel you forward and decreasing those that don't. Sounds like it should be easy, right? Especially because none of us are really living the lives that we want. But it's not, particularly the part about decreasing the things that don't push you forward. Who wants to hear they can't get bi-weekly mani's and pedi's even if saving is the goal?

Maintaining momentum means we have bad habits to let go of and positive thought processes to adopt if we are going to be intentional in finding success. It's also going to take extra effort to push through; but, it'll be so worth it. After reaching the goal, you can settle back down into a life balance and enjoy the success for a while until you set the next goal.

After you set a goal and map out your plan, there are a few things that will help you maintain the momentum to achieving that goal.

Finding The Time

One of the hardest things about accomplishing what we want in life is finding the time. We tend to put off what needs to be done until tomorrow or next week which turns into never. We all lead busy, complicated lives; we all have people we just can't say 'no' to. Then it seems when we do have time, we don't have the energy. 'Netflix and chill' has a whole new meaning when you're exhausted from being your awesome self. When we are too tired to devote energy or thought to anything, we nap or chill out in front of the TV. If you're already sacrificing what little free time you do have, where can you find the time to work on your personal goals?

There is no magic trick to carving out extra time. There is nowhere you can go buy huge chunks of free time to pursue all of the goals on your list. With work and commitment, your goal can be reached.

> ➤ *Start with your mornings.* Get up a little bit earlier and use that time to chip away at your plan. Clear the brain fog and get to work. Mornings are great because your brain will be working more quickly since it is refreshed from sleeping. Also, you're less likely to be interrupted by kids, your boss, your partner, or anybody else because, well, nobody will text at 5 in the morning.

> ➤ *Use your nights.* If you can muster up 30 minutes at night before bed, that would be a good time. No, you aren't refreshed, but you are still putting in the time and effort to get things done.

➤ *There's always lunchtime.* It's ok to pass on invitations from co-workers to go out to restaurants for lunch. Pack a lunch and sit at your desk to take an online course or write your novel. Doing something for you will serve as a midday refresher for the rest of your workday.

➤ *Use your commute.* If you are in a city where public transportation is the way you get to and from work, use that time to learn a new language or read a book about whatever it is that you are working toward.

➤ *Cut something out.* Take inventory of how you are spending your time. You will be surprised at pockets of 30 mins here and an hour there where doing nothing could be better spent. Scrolling through social media, reading celeb gossip, watching TV, and watching meaningless videos are time sucks that are robbing you of just that...time.

➤ *Block out the time.* Be just as intentional with the plan as you are with the overall goal. Dedicate blocks of time where you disappear to focus on what you need to. By scheduling the time, you are less likely to leave it up to chance, also encouraging you to maintain momentum.

➤ *Negotiate.* Can you talk to your boss about working an extra hour or two during the week for a half-day or day off on Friday? How about suggesting to your partner that if they handle kids and/or chores in the morning, you'll take care of them at night? Negotiating your duties will free up chunks of time to use.

Make A To-Do List

Organization, one of the great keys to life. A to-do list or plan is a master list of all of the steps required for you to see your end goal. Figuring out all of the tasks that need to be on your list can be somewhat of a struggle. That's ok. That's what Google is for. You can create and manage a to-do list on-the-go with specific goal-reaching apps or just the note app on your phone. That way you'll always have it and you can add or strikethrough tasks as you go.

After you write the list, prioritize it. If you are opening a hair salon, you can't buy the chairs before you acquire the property and you can't acquire the property without a business license. Do the research to know what needs to be done and in what order. Any stress you can eliminate as you chug away at your goal will help keep your momentum going. It also gives your tasks a place in your life.

Don't write a to-do list and hide it, make sure that it is easily visible or easy for you to get to and that you actually look at it. Half of the battle is knowing what it is you have to do that day or that week. If you need help remembering to check your list, put an alert on the calendar on your phone. These alerts can be set daily or weekly. You choose, but make sure you are choosing the option that will help you to be the most successful.

When you are constantly reminded of smaller tasks to do, it helps to keep your goal at the forefront of your mind which means you will be constantly thinking about it. Thinking about it helps you to create the vision in your head which brings about excitement because then you can see yourself accomplishing it.

Track Your Progress

It's not enough to have a master list to begin with, you have to keep up with your progress. You know how you go to a church that is striving to get a new building, they'll have the building fund thermometer posted somewhere for all to see? Tracking your progress is the same way. How can you celebrate your wins if you don't know how far you've come? Wait, I'm getting ahead of myself.

Somethings will be priorities in your #goaldigging, others not so much. Tracking what you've done will show the difference between the priorities marked off the list so you can get to what's next. Imagine how focused and determined you will be knowing what's ahead. It will give you a clear picture of what needs to be done and if you need to hustle a little harder because you're right at the finish line. Think about how marathon runners take off into a sprint as they get closer to the finish line. They know they are closer to the end and want to have a strong, quick finish.

Accountability partners are not just for trips to the gym, they can be very helpful in goal setting as well. Share your goal with a loved one, someone who you can be honest and upfront with. Let them hold you accountable throughout the entire process. Having someone other than yourself to answer to will also serve as a source of motivation.

You will be motivated by the encouragement they provide, as well as the desire not to let them down.

Celebrate Your Wins

As you mark things off your list, it's good to celebrate. Take a step back and look at your success. If you are constantly looking ahead at what still needs to be done, that can easily lead to burnout. You could get overwhelmed at what's on your plate versus appreciating how your hard work is already beginning to pay off. I know I'm guilty of thinking, *What's next?* We think that by jumping to the next thing, we're getting to the finish line quicker. And we are; but we are also doing ourselves a disservice by not patting ourselves on the back.

Celebrating along the way is a great way to stay motivated. Celebrating is also another way to track your progress because you are appreciating your hard work along the way. Take your accountability partner out for drinks, lunch, or even hot yoga (a little self-care never hurt anyone lol). Do something to highlight you are moving forward.

Be committed to the process of going after what you want. You know the goal you want to set, or goals – plural – if you're like me. Maintaining your momentum is crucial in creating the life of abundance that you see yourself having.

FRIENDS & FAMILY
Support

I am so blessed to have a tremendous amount of family and friend support. Not only does having a support system play a big role in entrepreneurship, but it also plays a big role in life period; whatever you are doing. The type of family that I come from has a loving background. Funny enough, but true, my parents are heavily involved in my life as if I were still a kid. They behave respectfully but are still involved.

Having their support is really important to me because it gives me a sense of security. I know they are people I can love and trust in my corner. Their advice is greatly appreciated, especially because I know my parents will not steer me wrong. It's funny, as a child I didn't want to listen to my parents. Now I highly value their opinions. Sometimes, I call my mom and demand she tells me what to do. It's so interesting how it went from, 'Ok Mama, you don't know what you're talking about,' to 'Mama, just say Chiara this is what you're gonna do!'

My financial service company is a family business. What do I mean by that? It was not a business I was born into, but I have hired relatives to work for the company and it has emerged into a family owned and operated empire. My cousins are tax preparers for my firm and my dad is the insurance adjuster for the firm. So with this, not only have I garnered family support, but I have made them a working part of my work-life. This is really big for me because it is bigger than them supporting me, it is also me being able to support them by offering employment opportunities and professional growth. Support goes hand-in-hand with scratch my back, I'll scratch yours. It encourages people to support you that much more because they see that you offer the same support you seek.

Everybody Won't Cheer You On

You can't expect everybody to support you. When you first start a business or announce a goal that you've already set into motion to reach, you instantly think, *My friends and family are going to be the first ones to cheer for me.* That is far from the case. The truth is, they may be the ones who need the most convincing. Most of my friends and family won't even let me prepare their taxes for them. Now, in all fairness, it could be that they just don't want me in their business, which is what I like to think. Realistically, it could be them looking at me as Chiara, their friend or relative and wondering why should they pay me to prepare their taxes for them. I have employees who come to me upset that family and friends won't let them do their taxes. I tell them not to let those close relationships suffer just because those who they expected to have as clients turn out not to be. They have to understand business is business, that shouldn't hinder personal relationships. Even though all of my family and friends have not supported my business, I am going on seven years strong with my company, Graham Financial Mall. That certainly says a lot about my credibility as an entrepreneur.

But what about a lack of support in personal relationships? This is perhaps even greater than the lack of support in business relationships because we all have goals that we want to achieve, though not all of us wish to open a business.

Don't expect everyone you know to support you. By this age, you should have already found that to be true. Expectations are dangerous territory. No doubt we all have unique expectations for the type of life we want to live, as well as who we want to become. Placing expectations on others is what will get your feelings hurt. Having unrealistic expectations most certainly will end badly – for you. The people who you are placing expectations on may not even be aware of what *you* expect *them* to do. You cannot expect just because you have a goal to reach or a business to launch that everyone in your circle will be supportive. It is unfair to them for you to place undue expectations on their level of support.

Ask yourself, 'Should they even support me?' Just because you launch a business doesn't mean they have to spend money with you. Just because your child is graduating high school doesn't mean they should come to the celebration. Just because you wrote a book doesn't mean they should read it. Since I am naturally a supportive person, I try to bring people in on what I'm doing. I make it my business to find ways to include others on everything I have going on. Again, this is finding a way to support them. A lot of people know this about me which can be a good and a bad thing. They know, Chiara is going to look out for them. If people need something, I'm usually one of the first people they call. And people rock with me because I rock with them.

What type of person are you? What is your give back? To be honest, you will have people wondering, what have you done for them lately. Remember that old Janet Jackson song, *What Have You Done For Me Lately*? Where do you think it came from?

Don't Play Into The Negativity

This is where having the right mindset as a #goaldigger comes into play. You can't let the motivation, or lack thereof, of others dictate how you live your life. Just because others don't support you doesn't mean your goals are not worthy of their support. When pursuing big dreams, it is common for others to question if you can do it...and if you will stick to it. Although you may have big dreams, it doesn't mean everyone does. Some people are completely happy with their lives and don't understand why you can't be. There is a difference between actively discouraging and being neutral.

Those who are seen as being unsupportive may just be neutral. Being unsupportive is not even their intention. Say your goal is to purchase your first home and you talk to your brother, who already owns a home, about it. You are excited and tell him how much it would mean to you to own your first home. Your brother listens but doesn't really give much feedback. You leave the conversation feeling dejected. However, from your brother's frame of mind, he offered you a listening ear which is a form of moral support. He may not have offered suggestions as to the direction you should go about making the purchase, but he also didn't tell you your dream couldn't be reached. In this scenario, rather than walking away thinking your brother is unsupportive, he could not want to overstep his bounds and is waiting on you to ask what you directly need help with.

Then, there are those who just flat out discourage you. I like to look at this scenario as them thinking how bossed up I will be once I accomplish the goal. I also think a part of them wants to discourage me because inside, they doubt themselves and find it hard to believe that I actually think I can do something and do it! This is their belief and they should deal with that on their own. It is more of a reflection of their small thinking than me not having what it takes.

What Is The Right Mindset?

Over the years, I've grown some thick skin and have changed the way I see their lack of support to keep it from bothering me. I had to do this to keep from getting in my feelings about it. I did not want my personal relationships to suffer with those who do not let me prepare their taxes or sell them their first home. I have come to understand that support comes in many different forms. This change in mindset came when I noticed someone close to me, who was not a client, post a flyer. Even though I did not 'work' for them, they still told others about my company, encouraging others to utilize my services.

Support is not just spending money with you, it's mentioning you, bragging about you, telling others about your accomplishment to highlight a goal that you have smashed.

Support is also a courtesy, it's something people want to do for you. If you don't have a supportive friends and family base, pay people to support you. Don't laugh, I'm serious. Think about it. If I was trying to get the word out about a special I was running for the upcoming tax season and I didn't have a network of folks referring my clients, I would pay people to repost my flyer or run a paid ad on Facebook. From a distance, you can't tell who is being supportive out of the kindness of their hearts and who is 'showing love' to get a coin. That's how business goes.

Here are a few things to remember about being supported...or not...

> *Being supported is a want, not a need.* Yes, we believe that our goals are worth shouting from the mountaintops, but they are our goals. Everyone else won't feel the same way. Understand that and experiencing less than supportive people won't hurt so much.

> *It doesn't make them bad people.* They may not be 'equipped' to be supportive. They may view things differently or even be jealous of your journey. It doesn't make you wrong, nor does it make them wrong. You just see things differently.

> *Seek outside support.* You may have to extend beyond your friends and family to get the cheering you need. This is painful to hear, but sometimes co-workers, neighbors, strangers, and associates will promote you more than those closest to you.

> *Don't ask more than they can give.* We each have a unique perspective on life-based on our experiences. Remember that their upbringing or current circumstance has a big impact on how they love and support others.

> ➤ *Don't try to convince them of your worth.* If they rock with you, they rock with you and you'll know it. Try not to pull out a PowerPoint presentation about the reasons why and how they can help motivate you towards your goal or others to utilize your products/services.

> ➤ *There are still others who will support you.* Energy will be wasted focusing on those who are not in your corner. Instead, refocus that energy to show appreciation for those who do.

> ➤ *No one will support you the way you support yourself!* If you believe in you, let it show. That kind of emotion is contagious, and it will spread! If you seem to be unsure of who you are and the value you can bring, others will be unsure if they should let you stand on your word.

Entrepreneurs...

There may be a genuinely good reason why you are not being supported as much as you think. If you aren't feeling the love you expect to receive, try finding out the reason why. Perhaps your products and services are not as appealing as you think they are. Maybe your flyer looks like a kindergartener put it together and would-be supporters think it's whack. Take a little time to go back to the drawing board to reflect on what you have to offer, what you are doing, how you present yourself, and how you are supporting others to see what it is that is keeping people from rocking with you the way you think they should.

I will say a trend that I have noticed in the business world is, everybody wants to be the face of their brand. It's like everybody wants to be famous or get attention. On the flip side, you have people who are so humble and want to remain in the background. Or they don't want their face associated with their brand because it could keep people from wanting to support due to not wanting to support the owner.

Social media has the world thinking we can all be the models for their clothing line, we can all put our faces on our books, and we can be the only people in their commercials. Think for a minute...do you know how the CEOs and owners of the household companies you support everyday look? I don't know how Christian Louboutin looks, and he is the founder of an internationally known fashion powerhouse. Attaching his likeness to the brand did not matter to him when he launched. Could it be that as a business owner, you are too much on the front line? You might not have all that it takes to be out on front street representing your brand. It won't take anything away from you to revisit whether or not you should be out in front of your new clothing line.

Is it necessary that people see the brand and automatically know it is your brand? Are your thoughts more narcissistic such as, yes people need to know that it is yours? I get it, with all of the resources that we have today and the effortless access to potentially reach millions on social media, it's easy to be that way. We've all seen success stories where people literally get instafamous in a year. They go from nobody to a person whose name everybody knows within the rotation of one calendar. Keeping that in mind, you wonder if the same glow-up can help you get a bag while making you instafamous too. Then, you may head down a dangerous road of doing things in real life just to be able to reflect them on social media.

This mindset has trickled over from influencers to business. This is one of the reasons I feel that entrepreneurship is trending right now, which is awesome! But owning your own business is also trending because of narcissism. Would you prefer to be the multi-millionaire behind the brand or are you happy being a hundred-thousandaire with your face plastered on everything. I already know you're thinking that I am the face of iGoalDig. What you don't know is that I've started businesses that people don't even know I'm associated with simply because I decided to find a more suitable image/person to be attached to the brand, other than myself.

Interestingly enough, as you become more confident in your business and goal-digging, you will notice others rally around you. Remember to show appreciation for others' goal-digging, not just solicit them to cheer you on. Support is a two-way street!

LEAP OF
Faith

You stand at a crossroads. You can go left continuing the path that you've been on or you can go right, exploring new territory. The thought of going right is thrilling and scary at the same time. Going left would be so much easier, and though going right will have its challenges, you believe it will be more rewarding. As you stand at this juncture in your life, you were driven by one of two things: feeling stagnant or desperation. Either you are tired of the way things are going, the way you are feeling with a run-of-the-mill boring existence, or your back is up against the wall and you might as well do it. Do what? Jump!

When it comes down to big decisions like a new mortgage, career change, getting into or out of a relationship, we always doubt the choice we make. We wonder...

- ➢ Is this the right decision?
- ➢ What if I don't have what it takes?
- ➢ What if I'm wrong?
- ➢ Is this something I can back out of?
- ➢ I don't really want to risk anything.
- ➢ I wish I could see into the future.

So...you make a decision. Even with doubt looming in your mind, the excitement of the newness takes over for a while. Perhaps you have stepped outside of your comfort zone because your gut is telling you to go in a different direction.

Most leaps of faith come from fear or desperation. We know that something in our lives must change; therefore, we take a wild, uncalculated risk to make ourselves happy. Our actions are somewhat frantic and hurried. There is not much thought put into them. The sink or swim mentality seems good enough to convince ourselves that we are doing the right thing. In this instance, the leap of faith is anything but. It is a leap of fear. The end result from this type of jump is rarely good causing us to move forward through life with caution, dreading the "leap of faith" that we took not realizing it was a leap of fear instead. You would never take a leap of faith again.

What if you could take the next leap of faith as just that, but limiting your risk of failure or burnout? If you could change your life for the better with greater odds of succeeding, still leaning towards faith? What if instead of closing your eyes and hoping to land on your feet, you aimed to guarantee success?

Before your next life-transforming leap of faith, let's better assess the situation.

How Do You Know When You Are Ready?

Plain and simple, when you seek change. When you are ready to change your life situation to reflect the vision of who, what, and where you see yourself in the future. When you know you need a shift in life as you see it daily, that's when you're ready. Most of us have a dream life. It's the way we see ourselves in our heads as we want to be, not as we are. We imagine this greater version of ourselves and know we have the potential to be that fierce badass, but we are afraid to transition into who she is.

For some, that dream existence is enough. They are happy only seeing this version of who they are in their heads, while they continue on in a mundane life. It is only when you are sick and tired of dreaming about it that you are ready to put action into becoming that woman.

You also know you are ready when the leap you take is of faith, but not blind faith. It is having faith in yourself. You have a lifetime of experience, skills, and knowledge to prepare you for the journey ahead. You also have the experience, skills, and knowledge of others who you trust to give their opinion. Their words can help nudge you in the right decision. Instead of shutting them out, use these resources.

Here are a few things to keep in mind when you are wondering if you truly are ready to jump:

> *Listen to your inner voice.* If your inner voice is telling you it's time to move, you may want to investigate that feeling. It's whispering to you to go ahead, do it, go this way. Subconsciously, you know you've been at a job too long because they won't promote you or give you a pay raise. You've been stagnant there for too long. Subconsciously, you know that you've been sitting on a great business idea that could be making you money while offering you a sense of happiness and accomplishment providing products/services for others. In a society where we look to others for validation, trust your gut. Your instincts should be louder than anything someone on the outside has to say.

➤ *Trust that instinct.* Have you noticed how eager you are to trust the word of coaches or experts? Don't toss your intuition to the bottom of the pile. Your experience and knowledge are valuable too. Again, a leap of faith is not a blind leap. You have to be prepared for multiple outcomes. Since you are operating in faith, not fear, you must trust yourself. You shouldn't put yourself in a position to fail. You should set yourself up for success. If anybody is going to look out for you...it should be you! You can feel your sense of purpose better than anyone else.

➤ *Your leap can be baby steps.* Ok, let's face it. Just agreeing to move on your feelings to reposition your life could be the leap, LOL! Maybe you are overly cautious, or in a situation where you can't just catapult yourself across the field quite just yet.

For instance, I have a friend who is a single mother of a teenager. She does not get child support and works two jobs to also help provide for her mother. Her father passed away when she was young and she has no other family. She can't just quit her jobs to launch her own business. The entire livelihoods of herself, her mother, and her daughter depend on her going to work every single day. But, she can take baby steps. She's started saving, fixing her credit, and doing research into the industry. In the evenings, she is perfecting her craft. That is a win for her. Small steps in the right direction will lead to the end result if you keep making them.

➢ *Leap with confidence...your new mindset.* You've got this! Replace the fear you have of the unknown with the possibilities of things to come. Remember that dream life you see every time your mind wanders? Focus on that. You're already visualizing a positive outcome. What does it look like? How does it feel? Who is there with you? Keep that positive energy to fuel your passion.

➢ *Find your supporters.* Everybody will not see your vision; then there are those who will. You can't make this journey alone and maintain courage while doing it. Find others who are interested in making the same journey or their own leap of faith. You can motivate each other to accomplish personal goals.

Are You Afraid To Fail?

The fear of failure, atychiphobia, is what keeps us from going after our dreams. No one likes to fail, but successful people understand that failure is critical in success. Albert Einstein said, "Anyone who has never made a mistake has never tried anything new." Failure elicits unpleasant feelings of confusion, anger, frustration, and regret. These same feelings come when venturing into waters unknown. The main motivation for not failing is to keep yourself from going through the gamut of emotions that come from not rising to meet your expectations.

According to Psychology Today, 10 ways to know that you are afraid to fail are:

1. Failing makes you worry about what other people think about you.

2. Failing makes you worry about your ability to pursue the future you desire.

3. Failing makes you worry that people will lose interest in you.

4. Failing makes you worry about how smart or capable you are.

5. Failing makes you worry about disappointing people whose opinion you value.

6. You tend to tell people beforehand that you don't expect to succeed in order to lower their expectations.

7. Once you fail at something, you have trouble imagining what you could have done differently to succeed.

8. You often get last-minute headaches, stomach aches, or other physical symptoms that prevent you from completing your preparation.

9. You often get distracted by tasks that prevent you from completing your preparation which, in hindsight, were not as urgent as they seemed at the time.

10. You tend to procrastinate and "run out of time" to complete your preparation adequately.

Address the fear of failure with preparedness. Preparing yourself before the leap will help to ensure your success. Use your supportive community to be a sounding board when you need to talk through emotions so you don't unconsciously sabotage yourself. Just as you can talk yourself into a win, you can talk yourself into a loss. Receiving much-needed reassurance from others can help to point out reasons for making this move that you may have forgotten about.

Michelle Obama spoke to a group of middle school students telling them, "Failure is a part of that whole process," Mrs. Obama said. "You just learn to pick yourself up. And the quicker and more resilient you become, the better you are." There will be disappointments along the way. You can't let them hold you back or regret making the decision. Failures should be seen as learning tools. Focus on what you can control. Brainstorm on ways to redirect your course to help safeguard success. Sometimes, that may mean going all the way back to the drawing board.

You're Never Going To Have All The Answers
Trying something new in life means just that...it's new. You are never going to have all of the answers you need to feel like, "Yes, I can do this. No sweat." With research and analyzing the options, you come up with a plan. Let's be honest. There is only so much preparing you can do. There comes a point where you've prepared and planned and prepared and planned and you just can't prepare and plan

anymore. You come to the realization there are some questions you won't get the answers to.

"What is going to happen next?" and "Will things work out?" are questions you'll ask yourself repeatedly. No prediction can define our exact outcomes. After all, experience is the best teacher. That means a lot of what you learn won't come until after you go forward with the plan.

If You Aren't Happy With The Leap

Undeniably, there is a chance that you will take that good ol' leap of faith and not be happy with the outcome. You won't be happy in that new job, you'll hate the new city, or the relationship will go down in flames. You will immediately wish you had not done it.

Guess what? You have the ability to change again. Keep moving, keep trying, stay on your journey to finding a way to get to that sense of inner peace and happiness that you seek. People who follow their intuition are fully aware of themselves and usually, move with intention. So, you can't go wrong by trusting your gut and making a move of faith even if it didn't work out.

You won't leap until you have set yourself up for success. What keeps people stuck is the fear of failure, losing or risking something. Landing in achievement after the leap will certainly reinvigorate your faith in yourself so the next time you want to try something new, it won't be foreign to you. You Got This!

ACKNOWLEDGEMENTS

When I first decided to write this book years ago, I struggled with exactly what I was going to talk about. My first thought was, *Do people really want to hear about me and my life?* I answered myself quickly, "Nope, not just yet sis. You're still building your story and legacy." So then I thought, *Ok well what the heck can I talk about because I still want to share my journey thus far and hope to encourage others as well?* After much procrastination, hesitations, and thought, I decided that I would just share what I strongly believe the keys to my success are and hope that these very keys can serve as essentials to other women like me to create her own success.

First and foremost, I want to thank my beautiful daughter, JadaMarie Samuel, for being my driving force and motivation to not only go ahead and write the book because it has been a long drawn out goal, but also that push needed in life to never give up because I now know who I do it for and that is her. Becoming a mom was my biggest blessing and at times when I wanted to say, "I give up on being an entrepreneur," I thought about my daughter and how I could never in life disappoint her or myself. Thank you JadaMarie for being my 'why.'

For my lovely parents, Clifton and Callie Graham, who support me in any and everything I want to do, thank you, thank you, and thank you. I give so much credit to my parents for pushing me as hard as they did and believing in me. I wouldn't be half the woman I am today if it wasn't for the loving background I come from.

My sister, Cristal Graham, who cheers me on in life because of how proud she is of her little sister. Although she is my oldest sister, she looks up to me in so many ways and a lot of what I do is for her. Her limitations in life are my motivations to do more in life because my success is also her success.

Jide, my spouse and best friend, thank you my love for all the encouraging words and never-ending support. You listen to all of my hair brain ideas and when I told you, "I'm writing my book for real this time lol," you cheered me on to do whatever it was I wanted and be the best at it.

To my supportive and creative friends, Jasmine Martinez, Keya James, Jervecia Whitaker, Jasmine Toomer and my cousin, Chardaris Cornish, thanks for your input and support every time I sent a random text needing your feedback and motivation. It meant more to me than you guys may have thought.

Carla Du Pont, my writing coach and editor, thank you for all your help and support. Collaborating with you to help me was one of the best decisions I've made.

Last but certainly not least, I thank God for the favor and blessings over my life and giving me the gifts and talents to be the woman I am today.

Finally, to my supporters and those who took the time out to read my book, I certainly thank you and it is completely humbling and inspiring to have the tremendous support I've received over the years. Thank You!